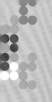

# COMPUTER
## ENGINEER
### RUCHI SANGHVI

LAURA HAMILTON WAXMAN

Lerner Publications
Minneapolis

*For Caleb, my computer wizard*

Lerner Publications Company
A division of Lerner Publishing Group, Inc.
241 First Avenue North
Minneapolis, MN 55401 USA

For reading levels and more information, look up this title at www.lernerbooks.com.

Content Consultant: Robert D. Nowak, PhD, McFarland-Bascom Professor in Engineering, Electrical and Computer Engineering, University of Wisconsin–Madison

Library of Congress Cataloging-in-Publication Data

Waxman, Laura Hamilton.
    Computer engineer Ruchi Sanghvi / Laura Hamilton Waxman.
        pages    cm. — (STEM trailblazer bios)
    Includes index.
    ISBN 978-1-4677-5794-2 (lib. bdg. : alk. paper)
    ISBN 978-1-4677-6283-0 (eBook)
    1. Sanghvi, Ruchi, 1982-—Juvenile literature.  2. Computer engineers—United States—Biography—Juvenile literature.  3. Women computer engineers—United States—Biography—Juvenile literature.  I. Title.
    QA76.2.S27W39  2015
    621.39092—dc23 [B]                                        2014015878

Manufactured in the United States of America
1 – PC – 12/31/14

The images in this book are used with the permission of: picture alliance/Jan Haas/Newscom, p. 4; © Dinodia Photos/Alamy, p. 5; © Tadek Kurpaski/flickr.com (CC BY 2.0), p. 7; © iStockphoto. com/Kameleon007, p. 8; © iStockphoto.com/abalcazar, p. 9; © iStockphoto.com/JasonDoiy, p. 10; © Steve Jennings/Getty Images Entertainment, pp. 12, 23, 24; © Justin Sullivan/Getty Images, p. 13; © Gilles Mingasson/Getty Images, p. 14; © Washington Post/Getty Images, p. 15; © Independent Picture Service, pp. 16, 20; © Ed Ou/Getty Images, p. 18; AP Photo/Eric Risberg, p. 21; © Steve Jennings/WireImage/Getty Images, p. 22; © Ariel Zambelich/WIRED/Condé Nast Collection, p. 26.

Front cover: picture alliance/Jan Haas/Newscom; © iStockphoto.com/Kalawin (background).

Main body text set in Adrianna Regular 13/22. Typeface provided by Chank.

# CONTENTS

## Chapter 1

Ruchi Sanghvi discusses online media during a conference in Munich, Germany, in 2013.

# FACING HER FEARS

When Ruchi Sanghvi was growing up in India, computers weren't a big part of her life. In fact, she didn't use them regularly until she went off to college in 2000. In 2004, a small, unknown social networking site called Facebook was just

getting started. Little did Ruchi know that she would go on to become a technology whiz and develop several key Facebook features that millions of people now use every day.

## A MAN'S WORLD

Ruchi was born on January 20, 1982, in the industrial city of Pune, India. Her father was a hardworking businessman who owned his own company. The company leased heavy equipment for industrial building projects. As a young girl, Ruchi dreamed of taking over her father's company.

Ruchi grew up in Pune, India.

Ruchi's father knew about her dream, but he warned her that the construction business was a "man's world." A woman would have a hard time getting into that kind of work. Ruchi could have let the fear of failing stop her from dreaming, but that wasn't her way. She was determined to do everything she could to have a career she loved.

When Ruchi finished high school, she told her family that she wanted to go to college in the United States. Then she could move back to India and apply her new knowledge to her father's business. Ruchi was eighteen years old. Her parents agreed but on one condition. They made her promise to come home and get married a year after she graduated. In India, it's considered very important for a woman to be married by the time she's in her mid-twenties. Ruchi's parents wanted to make sure that their daughter honored this tradition.

## COMING TO THE UNITED STATES

Sanghvi attended college at Carnegie Mellon University in Pittsburgh, Pennsylvania. She chose to study **computer engineering**. She also had an artistic side and planned to study set design for theater productions. She wanted to make time for both interests, but it turned out to be too much. In the end, she decided to focus just on computer engineering. She hoped her studies would lead to the kind of life she had been dreaming of.

Sanghvi moved to the United States to attend Carnegie Mellon University.

## Chapter 2

Computer engineers work with hardware (computer parts) and software (programs).

# FINDING HER WAY

As a computer engineering student, Sanghvi found herself once again in a man's world. She was one of only five women in Carnegie Mellon's engineering department. Sanghvi worked hard and earned a bachelor's degree and

then a master's degree. She graduated from Carnegie Mellon in 2005.

Sanghvi decided to stay in the United States for a while longer. Like many of her classmates in the computer engineering department, she got a job at a bank in New York City. Her job let her put her math and computer skills to use. Yet after she'd been at the job for just a short while, she began to panic. Working for a bank had never been one of her dreams. She wanted to help run a business, and she wanted to make a difference in the world.

After college, Sanghvi worked for a bank on Wall Street in New York City.

Silicon Valley is home to many tech companies, such as Oracle. Sanghvi joined Oracle in 2005.

## TAKING RISKS

Sanghvi knew she had a good job in New York. Giving it up to try something different was terrifying. What if nothing worked out? What if she failed miserably? But once again, Sanghvi didn't let her fears stop her. She flew to **Silicon Valley** in California. This area had become a booming center for the tech industry. One of Sanghvi's friends from college, Aditya Agarwal, worked in Silicon Valley at a company called Oracle. Oracle develops and manages **databases**. Sanghvi got a job there too, but she still felt restless. She wanted to find a job she felt passionate about.

## JOINING FACEBOOK

Then Sanghvi heard that a small start-up company was looking for computer engineers. The company was a social networking site called Facebook. Hardly anyone had heard of it, but Sanghvi had. In fact, she had used it herself. At the time, Facebook was open only to college students.

Sanghvi set up an interview at Facebook, but no one was there when she arrived. What she saw instead was a sign that read, Looking for Engineers. Someone finally showed up two hours later. He'd been working all night with Facebook's other engineers and had slept in.

The interview went well, and Sanghvi was offered a job. It was the fall of 2005, and Sanghvi had just become the first female engineer at Facebook.

## TECH TALK

"When I started out [at] Facebook, it had only 20 people. I saw it grow to a thousand employees and from five million users to over a billion users. I saw it evolve from a service that served college students to one that served the world."

—*Ruchi Sanghvi*

## Chapter 3

Sanghvi is not afraid to take risks in her career.

# WORKING AT A START-UP

To most outsiders, Sanghvi's decision to join Facebook would have seemed crazy. She had traded in a steady job at a well-known company for one at a struggling start-up. The owner of Facebook was a twenty-one-year-old college dropout named Mark Zuckerberg. The other employees at Facebook were also either college dropouts or recent college grads. They didn't have much work experience or many years spent as computer programmers.

What they did have was passion and a willingness to learn. So did Sanghvi. She knew that Facebook might fail, and that she could fail along with it. But she didn't let those worries stand in her way. Instead, she rolled up her sleeves and got to work.

In 2004, Mark Zuckerberg started Facebook while he was a student at Harvard University.

## LIFE AT A START-UP

In some ways, working at Facebook was like being back in college. Sanghvi and the small group of other computer engineers had to teach themselves how to build a social networking site from scratch. One of those engineers was her college friend Aditya Agarwal. He had also gotten a job at Facebook. All of them worked long into the night and slept in late. Sometimes they even came to work in their pajamas.

Mark Zuckerberg had a vision for Facebook. He didn't just want to connect five million college students to one another. He wanted his site to connect many millions of people from around the globe. Sanghvi and her coworkers had a big job ahead of them.

The atmosphere is relaxed and fun at the Facebook headquarters.

When Facebook first launched, a user had to click on each friend's page to find out information.

## FACEBOOK'S NEWS FEED

In September 2006, Facebook opened up to anyone in the world with an e-mail address. But the number of Facebook users didn't increase much at first. This was partly because Facebook wasn't all that easy to use. Back then, Facebook didn't have a home page with constant updates from friends and family. Instead, Facebook users had to hunt for information. They had to click on one friend's page to link to another friend and so on. It was like a complicated maze.

To solve that problem, Sanghvi and her team had been hard at work on a new feature called Facebook News Feed. This feature would allow users to see all of their friends' information on a home page. The home page would be updated every time a user's friends posted new information. That way, each user would have a personalized News Feed with updates from his or her friends and family. It was a huge task, but Sanghvi and her team managed to pull it off.

Sanghvi announced News Feed in a Facebook blog post on September 5, 2006. She excitedly told users, "Now, whenever you log in, you'll get the latest headlines generated by the activity of your friends and social groups."

News Feed allows users to interact in real time with updates from their friends.

## TECH TALK

"On January 25th, 90,000 people agreed to turn out for a day of revolution in Egypt, and they organized using Facebook. Never in my wildest dreams had I imagined that a product that I had built would impact the world in such a profound way."

—*Ruchi Sanghvi*

This big change inspired more people to start using the social networking site. It also helped make history by connecting people who were fighting for different political causes. For example, in 2011, thousands of people in Egypt used Facebook to organize protests. They wanted a new and fairer government. With the help of Facebook, their protests led to a revolution in the Middle East called the Arab Spring. Sanghvi also noticed that women from her own country were using Facebook to speak out for equal rights in India. Without realizing it, Sanghvi had helped connect people who were trying to change the world.

## Chapter 4

Facebook has become a popular site for organizing social change. Here an Egyptian youth updates a Facebook page for protesters in Cairo, Egypt, in early 2011.

# DOING MORE FOR FACEBOOK

Sanghvi had already done something big at Facebook, but she wasn't finished. The company had more big plans, and she wanted to be part of them. There was just one

problem. Sanghvi's parents were expecting her to keep her promise and return to India to get married.

Sanghvi took a break from Facebook to go home. Her parents helped set her up on dates with young men. Sanghvi used Facebook to find out more about them, such as who their friends were, what they posted, and what they were interested in. But she didn't want to marry any of them. In fact, she wasn't sure she was ready to get married at all.

Sanghvi was twenty-five years old. She knew that women her age in India were expected to get married, and she was afraid to break from that tradition. But once again, she refused to let her fears stop her. She decided to return to the United States and continue working for Facebook.

## TECH TALK

"I was afraid of the unknown. I was afraid of not following life's milestones—married at 25–26, and kids at 30. . . . [But since then] I've decided . . . to not be afraid of the unknown, because that's where the most exciting opportunities lie. [And I've learned] to raise my hand, and actually ask for these opportunities."

—*Ruchi Sanghvi*

# FACEBOOK PLATFORM

In 2007, Sanghvi led the development of a new product called
Facebook Platform. Facebook Platform allows **third-party
developers** to create **applications**, or apps, for Facebook
users. Many of these apps are popular online games that users
play on Facebook. Platform also allows Facebook to share
information about its users with the third-party developers.

Facebook Platform was a big hit with many users and
developers. By November 2007, developers had created seven
thousand apps for Platform. Over the years, that number has
increased by many thousands more.

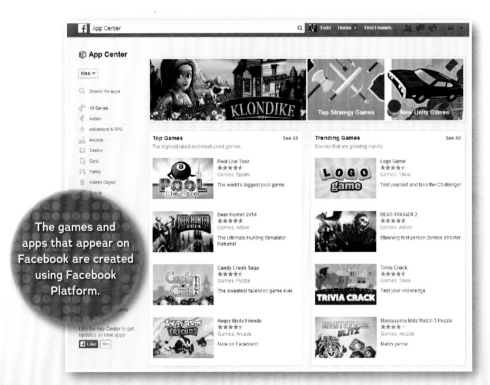

The games and apps that appear on Facebook are created using Facebook Platform.

## FACEBOOK CONNECT

While Platform was picking up steam, Sanghvi set to work on another product. It was a new part of Facebook Platform that became known as Facebook Connect. Sanghvi has said that it is one of the Facebook products she is most proud of.

Facebook Connect allows users to take their Facebook identity with them anywhere on the web. It allows Facebook users to quickly log on to outside websites using their Facebook accounts. In return, those websites are given access to some of the user's information. Facebook Connect was announced in May 2008. It became another one of Sanghvi's many successes.

## Chapter 5

Sanghvi *(right)* presents an award at the 2013 Crunchies Awards.

# TAKING
# NEW RISKS

Sanghvi's hard work paid off. In 2011, she received a TechFellow Award for her outstanding work at Facebook. The award included a $100,000 prize. Sanghvi planned to use the money to help other start-up companies.

But professional success wasn't the only thing Sanghvi found at Facebook. She also found love with her college friend and coworker, Aditya Agarwal. The two had been dating and decided to marry.

## A START-UP OF HER OWN

Things were going well for Sanghvi, but she was feeling restless again. She'd been passionate about building up Facebook, and it had become the world's largest social networking site. But she wanted to build a company of her own.

Engineering Leadership Award

Sanghvi (*second from right*) receives a TechFellow Award for her work in engineering.

Sanghvi attends the TechFellow Awards with her husband, Aditya Agarwal.

"This year, I made the most unconventional decision of my life. I quit Facebook. Everyone thought I was crazy. . . . I was working on these things that were impacting millions of users. So why did I leave? . . . I wasn't inspired anymore. And I didn't want to live out someone else's definition of success."

—*Ruchi Sanghvi*

As she had done in the past, Sanghvi decided to take a big risk. She quit Facebook and started a company called Cove with her husband. Cove developed software to help improve the way companies and other organizations communicate and work together.

## DROPBOX

A company called Dropbox liked what Cove was doing. Dropbox offered to buy Cove and hire Sanghvi and her husband to work for them. Sanghvi and her husband agreed to sell Cove to Dropbox in 2012.

JUSTWORKS

Sanghvi discusses ideas with team members at the Dropbox offices in 2013.

Dropbox provides **cloud storage**. This technology allows users to store computer files at a remote location. Users can then access and share their files through the Internet. Sanghvi became vice president of the company's operations, and her husband became the vice president of engineering. They shared their skills and ideas with Dropbox.

# EXPLORING THE FUTURE

Sanghvi had been working long hours for many years. In the fall of 2013, she decided to take a break. She wanted to figure out what she was passionate about and how she could continue to make a difference in the world.

## IMMIGRATION REFORM

As an immigrant to the United States, Sanghvi faced many roadblocks. She needed special permission from the government to attend college in the United States. To stay in the country after graduation, she had to keep a steady job. But finding a job can be tricky for immigrants. Many smaller companies don't want to fill out the extra forms needed to hire an immigrant. Sanghvi got lucky with her job at Facebook. Now she wants to help other immigrants. In 2013, she asked the US Senate to pass new laws that will remove these roadblocks and give US immigrants the freedom to find the jobs they want.

Sanghvi began investing money in other start-ups. These companies are developing new technology that excites Sanghvi. One of these start-ups is called Codeacademy. This free website teaches people how to write computer **code** in a fun and engaging way.

Sanghvi has spent her life taking risks and pushing herself to try to do new things. She has shown what a person can accomplish with courage and hard work. The question now is, What will Sanghvi accomplish next?

# TIMELINE

**1982**

Ruchi Sanghvi is born in Pune, India, on January 20.

**2000**

Ruchi leaves India to study at Carnegie Mellon University in Pittsburgh, Pennsylvania.

**2005**

Sanghvi graduates with a master's degree in computer engineering. In the fall, she lands a job at Facebook.

**2006**

Sanghvi helps launch Facebook News Feed, which attracts many new users to the site.

**2007**

Sanghvi leads the development and launch of Facebook Platform, which allows third-party developers to create apps for Facebook.

**2008**

Sanghvi leads the development and launch of Facebook Connect, part of Facebook Platform.

**2010**

Sanghvi marries her friend and fellow Facebook engineer Aditya Agarwal. She also decides to leave Facebook.

**2011**

Sanghvi and her husband start their own company, Cove. Sanghvi receives a TechFellow Award for her work at Facebook.

**2012**

Sanghvi and her husband sell Cove to Dropbox, and Sanghvi becomes vice president of operations.

**2013**

Sanghvi decides to leave her job at Dropbox and explore new career opportunities.

# SOURCE NOTES

6   Sophie Moura, "Ruchi Sanghvi: The Next Mark Zuckerberg," *Marie Claire*, 2010, accessed May 5, 2014, http://www.marieclaire.com/career-money/advice/ruchi-sanghvi.

11  Ruchi Sanghvi, "Digital Indians: How Ruchi Sanghvi Engineered Her Rise," interviewed by Soutik Biswas, *BBC News*, 2013, accessed May 5, 2014, http://www.bbc.com/news/technology-23881936.

16  Ruchi Sanghvi, "Facebook Gets a Facelift," *Facebook*, 2006, accessed May 5, 2014, https://www.facebook.com/notes/facebook/facebook-gets-a-facelift/2207967130.

17  Ruchi Sanghvi, "Ruchi Sanghvi: From Facebook to Facing the Unknown," YouTube video, 11:50, posted by "INKtalks," March 20, 2012, https://www.youtube.com/watch?v=64AaXC00bkQ.

19  Ibid.

25  Ibid.

# GLOSSARY

**applications**
software that runs on the Internet, computers, or mobile devices

**cloud storage**
the storage of computer data at a remote location

**code**
a set of instructions for a computer program

**computer engineering**
the science of designing hardware and software for computers

**databases**
organized collections of computer data

**Silicon Valley**
a tech center south of San Francisco, California

**third-party developers**
individuals and companies that develop software for another company

# FURTHER
## INFORMATION

## BOOKS

DiPiazza, Francesca Davis. *Friend Me! 600 Years of Social Networking in America*. Minneapolis: Twenty-First Century Books, 2012. Learn about the history of social networking, from telegrams to Facebook.

Goldsworthy, Steve. *Mark Zuckerberg*. New York: Weigl Publishers, 2013. Find out more about the man behind Facebook.

Wooster, Patricia. *Flickr Cofounder and Web Community Creator Caterina Fake*. Minneapolis: Lerner Publications, 2014. Discover how another successful woman in the tech industry helped start an innovative business of her own.

## WEBSITES

### Ruchi on Immigration Reform
**http://www.fwd.us/testimony**
Watch the speech Ruchi Sanghvi gave to the US Congress about immigration in the United States.

### Ruchi Sanghvi: Computer Engineer
**http://forgirlsinscience.org/women-in-stem/ruchi-sanghvi**
Read more about Ruchi Sanghvi and other impressive women in the STEM fields.

### Ruchi Sanghvi: From Facebook to Facing the Unknown
**http://www.inktalks.com/discover/75/ruchi-sanghvi-from -facebook-to-facing-the-unknown**
Hear Ruchi Sanghvi speak about overcoming fear and taking risks.

LERNER

SOURCE™

Expand learning beyond the printed book. Download free, complementary educational resources for this book from our website, www.lerneresource.com.

# INDEX

## ABOUT THE AUTHOR

Laura Hamilton Waxman has written many nonfiction books for young readers. She enjoys writing about people such as Ruchi Sanghvi who have shaped our world.